Negative Thoughts – A Guide to Overcoming Them

DR HITEN VYAS

CONTENTS

1 INTRODUCTION

When I was younger my life was crippled with worry and anxiety—primarily caused by my fear of stammering in front of other people. When I decided to help myself, I read books and began to learn about how my own negative thoughts were contributing to all the worry I was experiencing. I then learned how to change my negative thoughts, which changed how I felt and, subsequently, behaved in the world. By making changes to my thinking, I increased my own self-confidence, lessened my anxiety, and felt a sense of empowerment to act in the world in the way I wanted to.

The purpose of this guide is to help you change negative thinking you may be experiencing, which is holding you back in life. The first step in helping you do this will be through teaching you how negative thoughts arise in the first place by looking at the structure of how they are created. This will be covered in the next chapter. After this in Chapter 3, you will begin to learn principles of Cognitive Behavioural Therapy (CBT). You will understand how your thoughts can often contain errors in them and might not necessarily be true and will learn to practice a technique that will help you change negative thoughts into positive ones.

In Chapter 4, you will learn the importance of using experience in the real world as a way to deal with negative thoughts and as a way to look for validation for new and empowering thoughts you want to welcome into your life. You will learn how to identify problem behaviours, which you do to protect yourself, when in reality they just increase problems; then use this as a way to create experiments you can do in the real world to help change the way you think and feel about yourself, other people, and situations.

2 THE STRUCTURE OF HOW WE CREATE THOUGHTS

All thoughts, both negative and positive arise through a structure. In this structure, an event happens and you have thoughts in response to the event. The thought will then create a reaction in your body, which usually manifests in the form of unhelpful feelings such as worry, anger, anxiety, frustration, etc. Such responses are usually automatic and pretty soon they become so unconscious, it feels like you have no option but to react in unhelpful ways that leaving you feeling bad.

Example of Stimulus-Response in Action in the Real World

Jonathan had an incident at work the other day. He was organising a meeting at work that required a colleague to attend. So, he went to his colleague's team leader to ask if he could have some of his subordinate's time to attend his meeting. When he spoke to the team leader, the team leader responded in a way that Jonathan perceived to be aggressive. The team leader told Jonathan that his sub-ordinate was busy with the priorities of his own team and couldn't spare any of his time at the moment.

After this experience, Jonathan walked away and was angered by the team leader's response. 'How dare he talk to me like that, after all the favours I've done for him the past?' Jonathan thinks to himself.

In this case, Jonathan had experienced the stimulus-response model, which caused him to have a negative thought and corresponding negative feelings in his body. For instance, the stimulus was the team leader responding in a perceived aggressive way. The response was Jonathan saying to himself how he couldn't believe how this team leader talked to him in that way and then Jonathan getting angry.

Example of Stimulus Response in Action in the Mind

The stimulus-response model doesn't just apply to events that happen to us in the real world. As humans we can recreate events in our minds through remembering them and from this we can experience the stimulus-response model in ourselves. For instance, using the example of Jonathan above, after the incident, Jonathan keeps playing a movie of what happened in his mind when he got home. Jonathan thinking about the incident when he got home is another example of a stimulus and again he felt angered and hurt inside his body, which is an example of another response.

The importance of making interpretations of events

A key thing to recognise is that events that happen to us, either in the outside world or thoughts we have in our minds, never cause us to feel unhelpful emotions. It is our interpretations and meanings we have about events, which impact how we feel. However, our interpretations can often contain errors, which means that the meanings we attach to our experiences are not always correct. This is useful to know as it provides us with the basis to challenge negative thoughts.

3 ERRORS IN THOUGHTS

When we get involved in incidents and have thoughts in response to those incidents and when we think of incidents at a later time and again feel negative emotions inside our bodies, the thoughts we have seem so real. After all, we feel their effects in our bodies. However, the truth is that the thoughts we have often contain lots of distortions and errors. Usually we don't see these errors, unless we actually take time to analyse our thoughts. In this chapter you will learn about six types of errors you can have in negative thoughts.

Making it Personal

With this type of error, an incident occurs and you end up taking the result of it personally rather than looking at the incident objectively, to see if other factors might be playing a part in what happened.

Example

Joy works at a local charity shop, and a customer named Mary often comes in to chat. Joy has been very busy today and is feeling quite stressed. When Mary comes into the shop, and tries to start a conversation with Joy, Joy doesn't talk much and Mary perceives her as being distant. When Mary leaves, she blames herself for Joy's behaviour and tells herself, *I must have done something to upset Joy.* This type of statement is an example of personalising because Mary has incorrectly assumed that Joy was upset because of her.

How to Tackle Personalising

In order to handle thoughts where you've been personalising, think of alternative explanations of situations and events that have nothing to do with you.

Rejecting the Positive

Rejecting the positive involves taking an event or situation, which is positive but where you discount the positive aspect and make it into a negative event.

Example

Anne believes she is ugly. A friend recently told Anne that that she has lovely green eyes and wishes she had eyes like her. Anne believes her friend only said this because she felt sorry for her.

How to Tackle Rejecting the Positive

To work on this type of thinking error, you can consciously make effort to acknowledge positive comments made about you, by putting yourself first and believing that indeed a positive compliment that someone gives you, is because of you.

Strong Language

Strong language means the use of words that can affect you strongly emotionally, often in unhelpful ways. The words we use can cause us to feel bad about others, and ourselves, which can then impact whether we can tolerate certain situations, or can be used to react in calmer ways.

Example

Ryan is going out with his friends Mike and Martin. Mike tells Ryan that another friend named Jack is also coming. Ryan doesn't like Jack because Jack brags a lot about his money. Ryan says to himself, *I hate Jack. He's such a show off.* By using the emotive word *hate*, Jack creates a lot of anger in himself, which then results in him staying at home. Instead, if Ryan had said, *Jack's showing off is irritating. I just won't talk to him much*; he would have felt far less emotive and would still have been able to go out with his friends.

How to Tackle Strong Language

When you think of scenarios and find yourself talking about them out loud or talking to yourself about them, be mindful of the words you use and ensure you refrain from using terms that will inflame the way you are feeling. Instead, use words that will help describe events in the most neutral and objective way possible.

Using Feelings

Using feelings means when you use your feelings as evidence for why situations, people and yourself are the way they/you are. However, it is important to remember, that just because you feel something, it doesn't make it a fact, which can be used to explain why something has happened.

Example

Mary has just been reading an article in the paper about the increase in homeless children in her area. She then remembers how a fundraiser had knocked on her door the other day, raising money for a children's charity and how Mary refused to make a donation as she already supports a few other charities. Mary now feels very guilty and concludes that she is a very selfish person.

How to Tackle Using Feelings

If you notice your thoughts being taken over by strong feelings, a way you can deal with this is through noticing thoughts you have, which cause you to make certain facts. For instance, this could be, 'I'm feeling guilty, which means I'm a bad person' or 'I'm angry, which means I'm uncontrollable', or 'I feel frightened, a disaster is about to happen' and acknowledge that just because you are feeling certain emotions, it doesn't mean they represent facts and the truth.

Blaming

Blaming other people is something you can do when you are unable to tolerate that you might be responsible for a particular outcome.

Example

David's relationship with his girlfriend has been strained recently and he believes they are going to split up soon, as his girlfriend has had to travel a lot recently for work, and David has not seen much of her. David blames the struggle in their relationship on his girlfriend. However, he fails to acknowledge that he hasn't been making much effort to communicate with his girlfriend.

How to tackle Blaming

You can deal with blaming by considering who and/or what else could be playing a part in a particular situation. Also, think realistically and objectively about whether you could in fact be responsible for some of what has happened.

Jumping to Conclusions

With jumping to conclusions you can create a negative interpretation of an event without any facts that can act as real evidence for doing so.

Example

Janine is out shopping and comes across a friend who she hasn't seen for a while. The friend glances at Janine and looks away again quickly. Janine concludes that the friend ignored her because she didn't want to talk to her. In truth, Janine's friend didn't recognise her.

How to tackle Jumping to Conclusions

If you find yourself coming to a conclusion about how someone perceives or feels about you, then ask yourself how you really can be sure if this is the truth, or if it isn't just something you have imagined in your mind? Consider how realistic this conclusion really is and whether there are any hard facts to support it.

Conversely, if what you are concluding is about a bad event that will happen in the future, then remind yourself that you are creating a fantasy about what might happen. You can never know what will happen for certain until it happens, which will always be in the present moment and not in the future.

Exercise to Create Alternative Thoughts

In this exercise for one week, you will practice challenging the errors in your own thoughts you have in response to situations and consider new, alternative thoughts to help change the way you feel for the better. First, get seven pieces of A4 paper and write the following headings on each sheet, one for each day of the week. You will now have 7 Thought Recording

7

Forms, each with 6 columns.

Situation/event

What were your thought(s)?

How did you feel?

Errors in Thought(s)

Alternative Thought(s)

How do I feel?

Then follow the step-by-step guide below to do the exercise yourself. Also, read the example beneath the guide, which will give you an idea of what to do.

Step-by-step guide

Start the exercise on whichever day of the week you choose. On each day at the end of the day, for one week, use the Thought Recording Form you've drawn to do the following:

1. Identify a situation on the particular day that results in you becoming anxious, fearful, sad, angry, upset of any other negative emotion. Write it underneath the 'Situation/Event' heading.

2. What thoughts went through your mind because of the situation? What beliefs do you have about the situation? What do you say about yourself? What do you say about others? Write this down underneath the 'What were your thought(s)?' heading.

3. What emotion(s) did you feel because of the situation? Write these down underneath the 'How did you feel?' heading.

4. Find any errors in your thought(s) from Step 2 and write down the name of the errors (use the examples of the errors above in this chapter to help you).

5. Create an alternative thought (use the 'List of questions to ask yourself to help with identifying errors in your thoughts', which can be found after the

next example, to help you identify errors in thinking).

6. Note any changes in how you feel and write these down.

7. Do Steps 1-6 for any other situations throughout the day, which you had negative thoughts about.

Example

It is Monday and Paul has been analysing a thought he had in response to a request from his manager, who is asking Paul to lead a meeting at work with a new potential customer on Wednesday, as Paul's manager has been called away to another urgent meeting in London. He then examines how this thought made him feel. He also identifies any errors in his thought. After doing this, Paul comes up with an alternative thought that is more positive and notes how this new thought makes him feel. An example of how he has recorded all of this is in a Thought Recording Form is given below:

Situation/event

My manager Mark told me he needs to attend an important meeting in London on Thursday and asked me if I would lead the meeting, which our new client, Mr Xavier Dupont, will be attending.

What were your thought(s)?

I don't know much about this client and won't be able to create a good impression. The meeting is going to be a total failure.

How did you feel?

Anxious and worried.

Errors in Thought(s)

Jumping to conclusions.

Alternative Thought(s)

I'm only predicting what will happen. I can't be sure the meeting will turn out bad. Anyway, my colleagues will help by briefing me about the client before the meeting and they will also support me during the meeting.

How do I feel?

Less anxious.

List of questions to ask yourself to help with identifying errors in your thoughts:

Error

Personalising

Am I taking this situation, event, or someone else's behaviour too personally?

Am I ignoring other factors that could be playing a part?

Rejecting the Positive

Am I ignoring the positive or turning the positive into a negative?

Strong Language

Am I using certain words or phrases that are invoking strong emotions in me?

Using Feelings

Am I listening too much to my gut feelings rather than looking at the objective facts?

Blaming

Am I pushing all responsibility onto other people without objectively considering if I'm also responsible?

Jumping to Conclusions

Am I predicting what will happen in the future rather than just allowing it to happen?

Am I jumping to conclusions about what people are thinking of me without knowing for sure (for example, through asking them)?

4 USING EXPERIENCE TO CHANGE YOUR THOUGHTS

You can make a lot of progress just through analysing your feelings and thoughts in response to situations, and thinking of alternative thoughts to change how you feel for the better. However, another more powerful way to change your thoughts is through direct experience. When you actually have an experience, your whole mind-body experiences the incident and this enables you to doubt negative thoughts. Experience can allow you to get as much disconfirmation about your negative thoughts and beliefs as possible. For instance, if you think you will block up and not know what to say in a public speaking situation, then you might have an experience where you go into a public speaking scenario and do a test to see if you can say something when you stand up and speak.

Experience also always allows you to test out the validity of an alternative thought. For instance, if your alternative thought about talking to your colleague is that you *can* assertively voice your opinion about a specific work assignment, then you might test this out in the real world.

Safety Actions

In order to use experience as a way to overcome your problems, it can be useful to establish what your safety actions are. Safety actions are those behaviours you do, in order to protect yourself from fear, anxiety, or worry associated with certain situations. Ironically, over time, such protective behaviours only serve to keep the problem locked in. Further, these types of behaviours prevent you from realising that (1) the event you fear about might not even happen, (2) even if the feared event did happen you would find a way to cope with it and (3) the feared activity may make you feel uncomfortable. However, it is usually not as unbearable and horrible as you think.

Example

Rachel struggles with social events and avoids them altogether. In this particular case, her safety action is avoiding social gatherings. Although the purpose of her avoiding social events is so she won't look awkward in front of other people, the actual effect is not very positive as she will miss out on opportunities to develop her social skills. Also, she won't have the opportunity to find evidence contrary to her negative thoughts. Rachel does this through creating a table on a piece of a paper with three columns, each with the following heading:

Safety action

Avoiding social situations.

Purpose

Avoid looking awkward.

Actual effect

Missing out on opportunities to develop my social skills and no opportunity to find evidence contrary to my negative thoughts.

Exercise to Identify Safety Actions

In this exercise you will practice identifying three safety actions, establishing what their positive intention is and also what their actual consequence is. Create a table on a piece of paper with the following three headings. Like Rachel's example above, under each heading state a safety action, its corresponding purpose and the actual effect. Do this for three different safety behaviours.

Safety actions

Purpose

Actual effect

5 SETTING UP EXPERIMENTS

Now that you know how to identify safety actions—those behaviours that you do to protect yourself from some type of pain, yet have negative consequences—you can use these to create experiments to test whether a negative thought really is as true as you believe it to be and also test the validity of any alternative thought you have created.

Testing the Validity of Negative Thoughts

In this exercise you will devise an experiment to test out what will happen when you have a negative thought about a problem in real life, using the following steps. First, create a table with the following headings:

Problem

Negative thought in response to the problem

Prediction for the negative thought

Experiment

Results

Conclusions

Next, read each step a few times to get familiarised with the exercise, and read the example after it. After this, come back to Step 1 to try out the exercise for yourself.

Step-by-step guide

Step 1 – Describe the problem

In the first step, write down a problem that is impacting your life in a negative way. (Note it in the form of a safety action like those you learn about and practiced in Chapter 4). Write down your problem in the form of a safety action under the heading 'Problem' in the table you created.

Step 2 – Note your negative thought in response to the problem

In this step notice any negative thoughts you have in response to thinking about your problem and safety action. Write down the negative thought in the 'Negative thought in response to the problem' column.

Step 4 – Formulate a prediction

In step 4, predict the likelihood of what you are thinking may happen in the real world. Select a value between 0 and 100%. State the value for your prediction in the 'Prediction for the negative thought' column.

Step 5 – Carry out the experiment

Make a plan to test this negative thought in action. When you do so, be specific so you know what you are going to do, when you are going to do it, where you are going to do it and with whom. It is important to make the experiment as specific as possible and to ensure that it isn't vague. Doing so will help you to measure the results of the experiment, better. Write down all the specifics of your experiment in the 'Experiment' column in your table.

Step 6 – Review the results

In this step, do a review to see whether your prediction came true. Make a note on your table, in the 'Results' column of what actually happened, any thoughts you had during the event, emotions you felt, and sensations in your body along with how other people behaved.

Step 7 – Note down conclusions

In this step, in light of the results you obtained from your experiment, make a note of what you learned about your prediction in the 'Conclusions' column. Consider how you would change your initial thought in light of the new learning.

Step 8 – Carry out two more experiments

Using steps 1-7, create two more tables with the same headings and devise two more experiments to test the validity of two more negative thoughts that trouble you about two specific problems (safety actions).

Example

Joe's relationship with his best friend Dale has been difficult recently. Whenever Joe calls Dale for a chat, Dale always talks about himself and doesn't seem to ask much about Joe. This makes Joe think that Dale doesn't care about him anymore and this makes Joe upset. During the call, Joe often stops listening to Dale as a way to avoid listening to Dale talk about himself. Joe decides to carry out an experiment to test how true his thought that Dale doesn't care about him really is. See the experiment table Dale has created below:

Problem

Every time I call Dale these days, he seems to just talk about himself and I switch off while he is talking. I seem to be using this switching off as a safety action so that I don't have to listen to Dale.

Negative thought in response to the problem

Dale doesn't care about me anymore.

Prediction for the negative thought

My prediction that Dale doesn't care about me is 80%.

Experiment

The way I'm going to test this is through calling him tomorrow. If Dale starts to talk about himself, I'll interject and tell him about how I've been attending improvisation workshops and give Dale an opportunity to ask me about this.

Reviewing of the results

During my conversation with Dale, when I mentioned I had started improvisation workshops, Dale said this was interesting and asked me how long I had been taking the classes and where the classes were being held.

Conclusions

Dale does still care about what I get up to. My initial prediction that Dale doesn't care about me is now reduced to 40%.

Exercise to Test Alternative Thoughts

The purpose of this exercise is to test the validity of any alternative thought you create in response to a negative thought you have about particular safety action. The purpose of such an experiment is to not only disapprove your original belief, but also incorporate a healthier alternative thought into your life. Create a table with 8 columns, each with the following headings:

Problem

Negative thought in response to the problem

Prediction for the negative thought

Alternative thought to help with the problem

Prediction for the alternative thought

Experiment

Results

Conclusions

Then read the following step-by-step guide a few times and the example below it to get familiarised with the exercise. After you have done so, come back to Step 1 to try the exercise for yourself.

Step-by-step guide

Step 1 – Describe the problem

In the first step write down a problem that is impacting your life in a negative way. Note it down in the form of a safety action and write it in the 'Problem' column on the table you drew out.

17

Step 2 – Note a negative thought in response to the problem

In this step, notice any negative thoughts you have in response to your safety behaviour and write it down in the 'Negative thought in response to the problem' column.

Step 3 – Formulate a prediction for the negative thought

In step 4, predict the likelihood of your negative thought happening in the real world. Select a value between 0 and 100%. State this prediction in the 'Prediction for the negative thought' column.

Step 4 – Create an alternative thought

In this step think of another alternative thought which is more empowering and could be used to explain the particular problem or situation, in a more realistic way. Write down the alternative thought in the 'Alternative thought to help with the problem' column.

Step 5 – Formulate a prediction for the alternative thought

In step 5, predict the likelihood of your alternative thought happening in the real world. Select a value between 0 and 100%. Write down your prediction in the 'Prediction for the alternative the thought' column.

Step 6 – Carry out the experiment

Make a plan to test both the negative thought and the more positive, alternative thought in action. When you do so, be specific so you know what you are going to do, when you are going to do it, where you are going to do it and with whom. Write down all the specifics of your experiment in the 'Experiment' column in your table.

Step 7 – Review the results

In this step, do a review to see whether your predictions came true. Make a note on a piece of a paper of what actually happened, any thoughts you had during the event, emotions you felt, and sensations in your body along with how other people behaved.

Step 8 – Note down conclusions

In this step, write the results you obtained from your experiment; make a note of what you learned about from both of your predictions in the 'Result's column. Consider how you would change your initial negative thought and your alterative thought in light of the new learning.

Step 9 – Carry out two more experiments

Using steps 1-8, create two more tables with the same headings and devise two more experiments to test the validity of two more negative thoughts that trouble you and to test the validity of two alternative thoughts about two more specific events.

Example

Suresh has just lost his job after his role has been made redundant and has been given some redundancy money, although not much. He now fears that he won't have enough money to live on beyond 3 months. He avoids looking at his savings because he is afraid doing so will confirm his fears about not having enough money to live on beyond 3 months. Suresh decides to carry out an experiment to test the validity of this thought, and also of another alternative thought he has created. See the experiment table that Suresh has created below:

Problem

I've just lost my job and I don't have enough money to live beyond 3 months. I'm avoiding looking at my savings because it will confirm just how bad my financial situation is.

Negative thought in response to the problem

I can't look at my savings, because I'll see that I don't have enough money to live on beyond 3 months.

Prediction for the negative thought

I rate the degree to which I believe my thought that by looking at my savings, I'll see that I don't have enough money to live beyond 3 months, to be at 80%.

19

Alternative thought in response the problem

By looking at my savings, at least it will give me an idea of exactly what living costs I can cut down on, to make the money I have left last longer.

Prediction for the alternative thought

I rate the conviction of my alternative thought that by looking at my savings, at least doing so will give me an idea of exactly what living costs I can cut down, to make the money I have last longer to be at 70%.

Experiment

This evening I will take a look at all of my bank accounts, including savings accounts and calculate how much money is in each. I will work out my current expenses per month and see how far the money I have left will last me.

Reviewing of the results

By looking at my savings, I actually found an individual savings account, which has £9000 in it. I could use this amount in an emergency, which would last me for at least 6 months. By looking at my savings, I can cut some costs by switching to a lower tariff for my smartphone, remove my satellite TV package, which I hardly use, and switch to a cheaper Internet package. All of this will save me approximately £50.00 per month.

Conclusions

Looking at my savings was a good thing, because it allowed me to remember I had a savings account, which contains £9000 that I had forgotten about. I reduce the prediction that I can't survive beyond 3 months to 0% because with my current savings, I have enough money to live on, for at least 6 months. I increase the prediction that by looking at my savings, I can find areas where I can cut costs to 100%, as I can switch my current smartphone and Internet tariff to cheaper ones and remove my satellite TV package.

6 FINAL THOUGHTS BY THE AUTHOR

You have reached the end of this guide in which you have learned about how you can overcome negative thoughts. You now know how negative thoughts are created in the first place—through creating interpretations about events, and then experiencing corresponding, negative feelings in your body. You have also discovered how your negative thoughts can often contain errors. You have learned 6 different types of errors and practiced replacing negative thoughts about situations with alternative ones, which are more positive and realistic, to help you change how you feel for the better. After this, you learned about the importance of using experience as another way to change unhelpful thoughts. You learned two different types of experiments you can use to doubt and challenge negative thoughts and test the validity of alternative thoughts you want to welcome into your life.

I would like to wish you the very best in overcoming negative thoughts, increasing your self-confidence and living the life you want. If you have any questions, or need additional advice, then please feel free to send me an e-mail to hiten@hitenvyas.com.

7 OTHER BOOKS BY THE AUTHOR

How To Overcome Job Interview Anxiety.

How To Cold Call With Confidence.

Say No To Exam Stress.

Confidence With Women – How To Approach and Talk With Women.

Lessons in Unassuming Leadership.

How to Generate Innovative Ideas in 1 hour.

8 BIBLIOGRAPHY

Briers, S., 2009. Brilliant Cognitive Behavioural Therapy. Pearson Education Limited: Harlow.

Wright, J.H., Basco, M.R. and Thase, M.E., 2006. Learning Cognitive-Behavior Therapy: An Illustrated Guide. Washington DC: American Psychiatric Publishing, Inc.

9 ABOUT THE AUTHOR

Dr Hiten Vyas is the founder of Stuttering Hub Limited (http://hitenvyas.com), a company specialising in providing coaching services for people facing communication challenges. As a life coach, he is passionate about helping people increase their self-confidence and overcome fears related to communicating.

Hiten is based in Leicester in the UK and is available for private one-on-one consultation locally. He is available internationally and in India through telephone coaching. He is a Neuro-Linguistic Programming (NLP) Master Practitioner and uses NLP-based techniques in his coaching practice.

He has personally overcome some of his own deepest fears to lead a successful life. He has reached a position where he now believes that a person can achieve all they want in life, no matter how they communicate. He loves and embraces change. He is passionate about helping other people change and live fulfilled lives.

Hiten also has a PhD in Biomedical Information Systems from Loughborough University in the UK.

34867392R00019

Made in the USA
San Bernardino, CA
09 June 2016